The Unheard

The Unheard

Dr. Kumud Ramanand Bansal

DIAMOND BOOKS

X-30 Okhla Industrial Area,
Phase – 2, New Delhi – 110020
www.diamondbooks.in

ISBN: 978-93-7476-313-1

The Unheard

First Edition : 2025

Publisher : Diamond Pocket Books (P) Ltd.
X-30, Okhla Industrial Area,
Phase-II, new Delhi-110020
Phone : 011-40712200
E-mail : sales@dpb.in
Website : www.diamondbooks.in
Design & Type : Ravi Kumar Saini

The Unheard (Short Stories)

I dedicate this work

to

Amma & Pitaji

Foreword

The stories in this book were not written — they were overheard. Somewhere, a man and a mountain mocked each other. A devotee complained about his own life's wastefulness, forgetting that his life was equally inefficient. The wind ridiculed a stone and was nonchalantly rebuffed. And I, with no claim to originality, merely took dictation.

What you are about to read, then, is not a work of invention but of discovery — of the murmurs of the wind that carries old wisdom, to the silence between laughter, and to that eternal hum that the mystics of the East have always called the *soundless sound.*

For centuries, the East has taught through stories that refuse to behave. They do not explain; they *reveal.* They do not preach; they *play.* Whether it is a Zen monk who shouts to awaken a student, an ever-wandering Hindu Sadhu who smiles in silence, or a Taoist sage who answers a question with another question—the lesson, when it arrives, is not logical but luminous.

I have long admired this simplicity — the art of teaching through paradox, laughter, and childlike wonder. It is the opposite of the Western obsession with proving and defining. The Eastern teacher is less interested in giving you the truth than in dislodging your certainty. Her stories are not meant to make you agree; they are meant to make you *pause.* For in that pause — in that tiny crack of bewilderment — something real begins to shine through.

The Unheard by Dr. Kumud is a work that admires, above all things, the ways of the East—a wisdom that sidesteps the heavy-footed march of didactic logic, choosing instead to lead the way with paradox, laughter, and the disarming simplicity found in a child's question. Western logic divides the world into categories — mind and matter, body and soul, science and faith. Eastern wisdom sees all as threads of one vast tent, each interwoven with the other. It's this division into different, irreconcilable compartments that spawned the violence so much in the last 2000 years. This book contains the essence of Eastern wisdom — humility before the vastness of existence. Logic is a lamp; wisdom is the dawn. The lamp can guide us, but it cannot replace the sunrise. In the end, Eastern thought reminds us that knowledge is not about conquering the unknown, but harmonizing with it. When logic ends, silence begins — and in that silence, truth reveals itself not as an idea, but as peace.

Yunmen Wenyan (a Zen master in China from the Tang dynasty) once recited a story. A student asked a Zen master, "What is enlightenment?" The master spoke, "When you are hungry, eat; when you are exhausted, sleep." The student protested, "But everyone eats and sleeps!" The master smiled: "Not everyone eats *while* eating." That smile contains more philosophy than a hundred treatises. It is this essence of the East — the reminder that wisdom is not hidden in the sky but embedded in the everyday.

This book follows that path of wonder. Its stories are small doorways into vast rooms. They ask you not to believe but to see, to observe. You will meet donkeys that outwit their masters, beggars who speak like kings, and candles that dream of the sun. Each one carries a riddle that can only be solved by unlearning. Some of the stories will make you think, some will make you laugh, some will leave you uneasy, and a few may simply drift past you — but all of them will leave a faint echo, like a temple bell heard long after the wind has moved on.

There is a saying in the Upanishads: *"It is not by speech that the Self is known, nor by the mind, nor by sight."* Yet the same text then proceeds to teach through dialogue, story, and paradox. The contradiction is deliberate. The sages knew that even silence needs a voice. The stories in this book are that voice — trembling, uncertain, yet filled with a strange authority born of listening.

If you come to these pages seeking clarity, you may be disappointed. If you come seeking truth, you might find something subtler — a question that keeps returning like a sparrow to your window.

These stories do not promise enlightenment; they offer only a mirror. What you see there will depend on how still you can be.

In an age crowded with noise and opinion, perhaps this is what we need most — not another explanation, but another way of *hearing*. Somewhere between the donkey's bray and the saint's silence lies a music older than all philosophy. It is that music which these pages attempt to catch — faintly, humbly, but with love. With care.

So, welcome to a book unlike any other: a collection of dictations from the universe's enduring conversation with itself. May you, too, hear what Dr. Bansal heard. Let 'The Unheard' seep into you. This book is a little wonder which in incorporate its wisdom in daily life.

May it lead you towards *sat-chit-anand.*

Om Tat Sat.

Amit Agarwal

E-mail Id : cosmicgyaan@gmail.com

(Marathoner. Mountaineer. Author of Swift Horses Sharp Swords, A Never-Ending Conflict, Temple Treasures, Crossing Continents, Not Just Kohinoor)

The Unheard

There are moments in life when words stop pretending to explain and begin to become silent. 'The Unheard' was born out of such moments — brief flashes that appeared not as arguments or lessons but as whispers from the ordinary world: a bird's cry, a monk's laughter, the silence between two thoughts. Each story in this book is a small flame, lit not to burn but to reveal.

I have always believed that wisdom hides in plain sight — not in temples or scriptures alone but in teacups, shoes, crows, and clocks. The ancient Bhartiya Rishis said that Truth is "sat–chit–ānanda": existence, consciousness, and bliss. The Zen masters laughed and said it is just "suchness." The poets called it silence. I call it the pause between the question and the smile that follows. 'Unheard' gathers these pauses, dresses them in fables, and releases them back into the wind.

The stories were not written — they were overheard. Somewhere a philosopher's donkey brayed, a saint forgot his sermon, a candle complained to the sun, and I merely took dictation. I have long admired the simplicity with which the East teaches: through paradox and laughter, through a child's question that confounds scholars. In Bhartiya, Taoist, and Zen traditions, the path to understanding rarely runs through explanation; it moves through shock, wonder, or delight. 'The Unheard' follows that path.

These parables are not moral lessons. They are mirrors — and mirrors never preach. They simply reflect the reader's own face, sometimes with affection, sometimes with mischief. The monk's wisdom, the fool's mistake, the child's question — each is you, seen from a slightly different window. When you laugh at the "Drunk Master," or the "Wise Donkey," or the "Robot's Prayer," perhaps something inside is laughing at its own disguises.

I created this book not as a scholar but as a witness to life's absurd balance. The sacred and the ridiculous share the same stage: Gods forget their passwords; saints oversleep; philosophers wear golden slippers; the wise barber doubles his pay for honesty. Beneath their humor lies compassion — a reminder that enlightenment does not need solemn faces. If truth is a flame, laughter is its oxygen.

The form of 'The Unheard' is deliberately short. Brevity, I have learned, sharpens perception. In few lines, a whole universe can unfold, provided one listens between the lines. Each parable is a doorway, not a destination. They do not claim to answer life's questions; they only rearrange them until a new light passes through. Sometimes, that light is laughter; sometimes, a sigh; sometimes, a stillness that has no name.

Modern life, crowded with noise and notifications, leaves little space for stillness. Yet even a second of insight can change the texture of a day. That is what I wish for these stories — that they become small interruptions in the reader's routine, like sudden rain on a busy road. We live surrounded by algorithms that predict us, markets that measure us, and machines that mimic our emotions. In such an age, wisdom must become quick, portable, and precise — like a spark.

Many traditions have inspired these pages: the parables of the Buddha, the dialogues of Lao Tzu, the koans of Zen masters, the irony of Kabir, the tenderness of Sufi poets. But their spirit is one: that truth cannot be told, only hinted. Each tale is a gesture toward something beyond itself — an awakening that begins as amusement.

The reader is invited to "hear" that which is unheard. Read one and let it settle. Some will make you laugh immediately; others may puzzle you for days. That delay is the real teaching. Wisdom is not in the words; it grows in the silence that follows them.

I owe gratitude to every nameless encounter that became a metaphor — to the candle that flickered, to the dog that slept in philosophy, to the river that answered back. Gratitude, too, to those who have preserved humor in their pursuit of truth, for without humor, wisdom hardens into doctrine.

Laughter softens it back into life.

If these parables seem contradictory, they are meant to be. The universe is too vast to fit one interpretation. Contradictions remind us that truth is not linear; it is circular, like the dance of the planets or the breath that returns to itself.

Perhaps someday, a reader will find one story that lingers — a sentence that echoes in the mind during a quiet walk, a line that suddenly makes sense years later. That will be the real completion of this book. Until then, 'The Unheard' remains unfinished, as all wisdom should be.

Every writer begins as a reader of the invisible. Before I wrote these parables, I was simply listening—to the hum of existence that often hides behind routine. A conversation overheard in a tea stall, a crow's insolent caw at dawn, a child's absurd yet perfect question—these were my scriptures. The world spoke in riddles; all I did was translate them into stories short enough to fit between two breaths.

I have always felt that our age suffers not from lack of knowledge but from lack of wonder. Knowledge multiplies; wonder withers. The faster we learn, the less we pause to marvel. I wanted 'The Unheard' to restore that pause—to bring back the gentle art of astonishment. The shortest parables often burn the brightest because they leave space for the reader's imagination to enter. When a story ends abruptly, it begins again inside the reader's thought.

That continuation is where meaning takes birth.

My childhood was filled with storytellers who never called themselves writers: a grandmother who turned every meal into a fable; a village teacher who saw metaphors in dust storms; a traveling Sadhu who laughed at logic and lived on riddles. From them I learned that language need not always explain—it can simply 'evoke.' The best stories are like incense; they fade, but the fragrance remains.

I also learned from silence. In the still moments between words, the heart becomes its own narrator. The mystics of every tradition knew this secret—that silence is the final punctuation of truth. Kabir's couplets, Lao Tzu's paradoxes, the Buddha's pauses before speech, Christ's silence before Pilate—all remind us that insight ripens in quietude, not argument.

In this collection, laughter walks beside wisdom. Humor, when it matures, becomes compassion. A saint who laughs at himself is closer to liberation than one who frowns at others. Each spark in this book hides a smile—a reminder that truth, if it cannot dance, soon dies of solemnity. The divine itself seems to enjoy irony: it hides eternity inside a second, infinity inside a grain of sand.

There is also an undercurrent of humility in these tales. They do not claim authority; they invite companionship. I see the reader not as a disciple but as a fellow traveler. Together we stand by the roadside of existence, watching absurdities unfold with equal amusement and empathy. If, while reading, you find yourself smiling, pausing, or simply breathing a little slower, the purpose of 'Unheard' is fulfilled.

We live in an age where technology amplifies voices but often diminishes meaning. Our devices respond faster than our hearts. We scroll past wisdom and mistake data for depth. In such times, storytelling becomes resistance—a quiet rebellion that reclaims slowness, contemplation, and tenderness. Every parable in 'The Unheard' is an invitation to reclaim your own inner stillness, to rediscover that you can laugh and awaken at the same time.

Some readers may wonder why the stories mix ancient imagery with modern absurdities—robots, smartphones, ministers, algorithms. The reason is simple: the human condition has not changed, only its costumes have. Greed, pride, confusion, longing, love—these are ancient software running on new devices. The parables hold up a mirror to this continuity, reminding us that enlightenment is not a museum artifact; it is an everyday possibility.

In writing these stories, I found that humor and humility share a common root. Both require one to step aside from the ego. To laugh at oneself is to bow to the cosmic joke that we call life. In that laughter, the gap between the sacred and the profane disappears. The saint snores, the fool becomes wise, the child turns philosopher. 'The Unheard' celebrates these moments of reversal—the little earthquakes that loosen the rigid soil of our assumptions.

I owe my gratitude to the countless teachers who never met me: to the laughter of children, the patience of rivers, the sarcasm of crows, and the occasional honesty of silence. They have been my true mentors. Every story is, in a sense, an offering to them.

Finally, to the reader—thank you for listening to the unheard and melting it into your own world. May they fall where they are needed most: on the damp wood of fatigue, on the cold hearth of habit, or upon the dark corridors of thought. May they kindle without consuming, light without blinding, and vanish only after warmth remains.

For wisdom, after all, is not a fire to possess; it is a light to pass on.

Dr. Kumud Ramanand Bansal

Vikram Samvat 2082
Kartik Shukl Prabodhini Akadashi
November 1, 2025

The Empty Teacup

A scholar asked the monk for wisdom. The monk poured tea until the cup overflowed.
"Why waste tea?" cried the scholar.
The monk said, "Why waste truth on a full head?"

Punchline: Only an empty cup can hold wisdom.

The Sleeping Buddha

A man prayed at a Buddha statue.
A bird built a nest on its head.
The man got angry.
The Buddha kept sleeping.

Punchline: Peace keeps sleeping when devotion demands drama.

The Monk's Shoes

A disciple polished the master's sandals daily.
One day, the master walked barefoot.
The disciple cried, "What of my devotion?"
The master smiled, "Polish your own feet."

Punchline: True service begins when praise ends.

The River's Question

The river asked the bridge, "Why do you cross me?"
The bridge replied, "Why do you run under me?"
Punchline: Every question reflects the path it travels.

The Burning Incense

A devotee complained: "My prayers vanish like smoke!"
The sage replied, "So does life. Does that make it useless?"

Punchline: That which vanishes is often what was offered.

The Stone and the Wind

The wind mocked the stone: "You cannot move!"
The stone replied, "You cannot stay."

Punchline: Stability and motion trade insults like friends.

The Ant and the Mountain

The ant said, "I will climb you."
The mountain replied, "I will wait."

Punchline: Small resolve meets patient time—and both win.

The Master's Laughter

A disciple asked, "What is truth?"
The master burst into laughter.
The disciple became enlightened.
Or maybe deaf.
Punchline: Sometimes a laugh is the shortest route to truth.

The Empty Scroll

A king asked for the greatest scripture.
The sage gave him a blank scroll.
The king grew angry.
The sage said, "Now you have space to write your own truth."

Punchline: When words fail, the blank page becomes a teacher.

The Talking Fish

A fisherman caught a fish that spoke: "Spare me, and I'll tell you wisdom."
The fisherman replied, "I'm hungry. Talk after dinner."

Punchline: Wisdom waits politely until appetite is sated.

The Candle in the Storm

A disciple protected a candle in the wind.
The master blew it out.
"Why?" asked the disciple.
"To show you the sun was already rising."

Punchline: Only the wind can show the sun's patience.

The Beggar's Gift

A beggar gave a coin to a king.
The king asked, "Why give me what I have plenty of?"
The beggar said, "To prove you are poorer than me."

Punchline: Richness is measured by what you can still give away.

The Drowning Student

A master held a student's head underwater.
The student gasped for air.
"Why do you torture me?"
"When you want truth like you wanted air, come back," said the master.

Punchline: Desire for truth must hurt like air to be remembered.

The Snoring Monk

Disciples meditated in silence. One monk snored loudly.
They complained to the master.
The master said, "At least he breathes honestly."

Punchline: Honest breath is better than hypocritical silence.

The Echo

A man shouted at the mountains.
The echo mocked him.
He shouted louder.
The mountain laughed.

Punchline: Shout less—let the mountain keep its laughter.

The Old Tree

A disciple asked, "How do I find enlightenment?"
The master pointed to a tree.
The disciple stared.
Nothing happened.
The master said, "Exactly."

Punchline: Enlightenment grows where impatience sits quietly.

The Drunk Master

The disciples found their master drinking wine.
"Is this enlightenment?" they asked.
The master hiccupped: "Better than your seriousness."

Punchline: A hiccup often teaches what solemn looks cannot.

The Talking Corpse

A corpse rose during cremation and asked, "What is life?"
The priest fainted.
The fire answered by burning anyway.

Punchline: Some answers arrive when silence burns the loudest.

The Last Question

On his deathbed, the sage whispered, "I don't know."
The disciples gasped.
He smiled,
"That's why I'm free."
Punchline: Not knowing is the final freedom.

The Empty Bowl

The monk held up his begging bowl.
"It is empty," said the disciple.
"Good," said the monk. "Now it can be filled."

Punchline: An empty bowl invites everything that follows.

The Window

Student: "How do I control anger?"
Master: "Try controlling the wind."
Student: "Impossible!"
Master: "Then open the window."
Punchline: You cannot control the wind—open the window instead.

The Talking Corpse

At his own funeral, the dead man sat up.
"Why are you crying?" he asked.
The priest said, "Because we can't do this for ourselves."

Punchline: We weep because some chores cannot be done for us.

The Endless Queue

A man stood in a government line for enlightenment.
After years, he reached the counter.
The clerk said, "Wrong queue. Enlightenment was self-service."

Punchline: Enlightenment is the self-service counter.

The Coin

Disciple: "What is wealth?"
Sage: "The side of a coin you never see."

Punchline: Wealth plays on sides we rarely see.

The Door

Seeker: "Where is truth?"
Master: "Behind the door."
The seeker opened it. Nothing there.
Master: "That's the truth."

Punchline: Truth often stands behind an empty room.

The Book

Reader: "I've finished 1,000 books."
Monk: "Good. Now finish your mind."

Punchline: Finish your mind after you finish your books.

The Shoe

Man: "Why do my shoes wear out?"
Cobbler: "Because roads are wiser than you."

Punchline: Roads teach what shoes only wear.

The Crow

Boy: "Why does the crow caw?"
Old man: "So fools like us can ask why."

Punchline: Some questions exist simply to remind us we asked.

The Candle

Disciple: "What is faith?"
Guru: "A candle in daylight. The world laughs, but you still light it."

Punchline: Light a candle even if the world laughs.

The Rope

Child: "What is fear?"
Father: "A rope mistaken for a snake. You scream until the light is lit."

Punchline: Fear is a rope until you see the snake for what it is.

The Key

Man: "How do I find freedom?"
Saint: "Check your own pocket first."

Punchline: Freedom begins in your own pocket.

The Broken Clock

A temple clock struck thirteen at midnight.
Villagers panicked.
The saint laughed: "At least once, the liar spoke beyond time."

Punchline: Even broken truths can surprise at midnight.

The Holy Cow

A cow wandered into a temple.
Priests bowed to her.
She chewed plastic bags in response.

Punchline: Reverence sometimes forgets the practical.

The Silence

Scholar: "What is the highest sound?"
Hermit: "The one that shuts you up."

Punchline: The highest sound is the one that stills you.

The Bridge

A man built a bridge to heaven.
Nobody used it.
They all preferred elevators to malls.

Punchline: Not every bridge leads to heaven—some lead to convenience.

The Judge's Dream

A judge dreamt criminals were free, and saints were in jail.
He woke up sweating.
In court, nothing seemed different.

Punchline: Dreams rearrange justice until morning corrects them.

The Eternal Traffic Jam

A devotee asked God, "Why don't you answer prayers?"
God replied, "They're stuck in traffic, like your cars."

Punchline: Prayers misplace themselves where our cars do.

The Cup of Emptiness (Taoist)

A disciple asked, "Why does the cup hold tea?"
The master lifted the cup and tapped it.
"Because it is empty."
The disciple frowned. "Then why is my mind so heavy?"
The master overturned the cup; a drop of tea spilled to the earth.
"Begin with a single drop."

Punchline: A cup holds because it begins as nothing.

The Drowning Saint

A saint who preached detachment slipped into a river.
He screamed, "Save me, I'm not ready!"
The river said, "Neither am I."

Punchline: Even rivers admit they're not ready for all of us.

The Voting Booth

People voted for truth.
The ballot machine declared: "Error 404—Not Found."

Punchline: When truth is swiped, systems return Error 404.

The Mirror of Kabir

A man looked into a mirror.
He saw not himself, but the whole village.
He shouted, "Who are you?"
The mirror replied, "Everyone you refuse to see."

Punchline: You are everyone you refuse to see.

The Lute of Harmony (Confucian)

A disciple brought a lute to his master.
He tightened one string until it snapped. Another hung too loose and made no sound.
The master tuned both carefully and played a melody.
"Do you hear? Harmony is not perfection, but balance.
And life too must be tuned."

Punchline: Balance makes music out of imperfect strings.

The Bamboo Silence (Zen)

A monk asked, "How may I find stillness?"
The master closed his eyes. Outside, the wind stirred the bamboo, swaying and whispering.
The monk said, "The wind is noisy."
The master replied, "Then be bamboo."

Punchline: If the wind is loud, be bamboo and sway.

The Barber's Truth

A king asked his barber, "How does my crown look?"
The barber whispered, "Better when your head behaves."
The king doubled his pay, and banned mirrors.

Punchline: A crown looks better when the head behaves.

The Market Prophet

A man shouted, "The world will end tomorrow!"
The crowd panicked, markets crashed, and he made a fortune selling candles.
The world didn't end.
But his career in prophecy began.

Punchline: Prophecy thrives where panic is profitable.

The Wise Woman's Shoe

A villager complained, "My shoe is torn."
The wise woman said, "Then your toes will learn the weather."
He laughed, fixed the shoe, and discovered gratitude was cheaper than leather.

Punchline: Torn shoes teach weather better than lectures.

The Owl and the Mirror

An owl asked a mirror, "Why do you never praise my wisdom?"
The mirror replied, "Because you never ask a foolish question."

Punchline: Mirrors answer only foolish questions when asked.

The Scholar's Donkey

A scholar rode his donkey backwards.
People laughed, "Why not face forward?"
He said, "Better the donkey look foolish than me."
The donkey brayed. Nobody knew who won.

Punchline: Better a foolish ride than an arrogant scholar.

The Beggar's Complaint

A beggar said, "The world is unfair!"
A passerby dropped a coin.
The beggar sighed, "Still unfair. Why only one?"
Justice is never enough when appetite is endless.

Punchline: One coin rarely cures a complaint.

The Miser's Feast

A miser invited guests but served water and dry bread.
When asked why, he said, "I want praise for simplicity."
The guests left hungry, but he felt full—of himself.

Punchline: Praise for simplicity is cheapest when you can afford it.

The Tailor's Needle (Persian twist)

A tailor pricked his finger and cursed the needle.
The needle whispered, "I carry your wisdom in every stitch."
He smiled. Pain became part of the design.

Punchline: Every stitch carries the seam of your wisdom.

The Astrologer's Umbrella

An astrologer predicted clear skies.
When it rained, he said, "The stars were joking."
He sold umbrellas at double price.
Faith pays better than science.

Punchline: When stars joke, businessmen profit in the rain.

The Farmer's Clock

A farmer bought a fancy clock that chimed every hour.
By noon, he was exhausted—counting instead of working.
He threw it away and said, "Best clock is the sun."

Punchline: Sun-time costs no attention and pays all wages.

The Fisherman's Net

A tourist asked a fisherman, "Why don't you fish more?"
The fisherman said, "Why don't you rest more?"
They stared at each other.
The sea laughed.

Punchline: Ask why he rests; he may ask why you fish.

The Caged Parrot

A parrot in a golden cage sang loudly, "Freedom!"
A crow outside said, "Then fly."
The parrot replied, "Too shiny here to leave."
Punchline: Shiny cages make timid birds sing of freedom.

The Old Lantern

A lantern asked, "Why am I never lit anymore?"
The moon said, "Because I borrowed your job."
Punchline: Even forgotten lamps keep a small pride.

The Painter's Cat

A painter scolded his cat for paw prints on the canvas.
The buyers loved it.
The painter meowed and called it "modern art."

Punchline: Art is what happens when accidents find buyers.

The Sage and the Shoes

A sage wore torn shoes.
A rich man mocked, "Where's your dignity?"
The sage said, "I walk on earth, not on opinions."

Punchline: Walk the earth; leave opinions to pavements.

The Wise Barber

A king asked his barber, "What do people say of me?"
The barber whispered, "They say I'm brave—for answering you honestly."

Punchline: Honesty earns double pay, if not comfort.

The Potter's Bowl

A cracked pot carried water, dripping along the path.
Flowers bloomed where it leaked.
The pot wept, "I am useless."
The potter said, "You watered beauty."

Punchline: Cracks water the path where beauty grows.

The Owl's Complaint

The owl said, "Humans call me wise, yet fear me."
The crow laughed, "That's wisdom—never work for your PR team."

Punchline: Wisdom needs no PR—only night and a quiet tree.

The Hermit's Silence

A villager begged, "Teach me wisdom!"
The hermit stayed silent.
The villager grew angry and left.
The hermit whispered, "Lesson complete."

Punchline: Silence sometimes teaches by absence.

The Carpenter's Hammer

A hammer boasted, "I build houses!"
The wood replied, "And I live in them."
Both were silent before the rain.

Punchline: Both builder and built fall silent before the rain.

The Old Mirror

A lady polished her mirror until it cracked.
She sighed, "Perfection breaks things faster than time."

Punchline: Perfection polishes until it breaks itself.

The Hungry Monk

A monk preached renunciation all day.
At night he hid sweets under his pillow.
Enlightenment sometimes smells of sugar.

Punchline: Even renunciation occasionally smells of sugar.

The Goat and the Scholar

A goat ate the scholar's manuscript.
The scholar cried, "My wisdom is lost!"
The goat burped, "Now it's digested."

Punchline: What's chewed often becomes more digestible wisdom.

The Lazy Saint

A saint slept through the temple prayers.
When asked why, he replied, "Even God naps in between requests."

Punchline: Even the divine deserves a nap.

The Chessboard King

A king played chess and lost to a peasant.
He flipped the board and shouted, "Game over!"
History is written by kings, not pawns.

Punchline: When kings flip boards, history rewrites losers as lessons.

The Empty Jar

A teacher showed a jar full of stones.
"Full?" he asked.
Students said, "Yes."
He poured in sand, then tea.
"Now it's truly full," he smiled.

Punchline: Fullness often depends on what else you pour in.

The Candle and the Moth

The moth said, "Your light is divine!"
The candle whispered, "It kills you."
Devotion rarely reads the warning label.

Punchline: Devotion rarely reads the warning label.

The Merchant's Prayer

A merchant prayed: "God, bless my business."
God replied, "Then stop cheating your customers."
The merchant changed gods.

Punchline: Prayers to prosper must first stop cheating.

The Cloud's Laughter

A cloud wept, "Everyone hates my rain!"
The farmer clapped, "Everyone loves my harvest."
Perspective is simply weather in disguise.

Punchline: Weather is simply perspective in motion.

The Dog at the Palace

A dog entered a palace and barked at the mirrors.
Seeing hundreds of dogs barking back, he fainted.
Not enemies—only reflections.

Punchline: Reflections confuse even palace dogs.

The Weaver's Thread

A thread asked, "Am I important?"
The weaver replied, "Without you, the cloth is naked."
Threads never ask again.

Punchline: Threads stop asking once they know they clothe the world.

The Philosopher's Shoes

A philosopher walked barefoot on thorns.
People said, "How painful!"
He smiled, "Every step is free education."

Punchline: Pain is education when you walk barefoot on truth.

The Baker's Secret

A baker sold stale bread as "aged artisan loaves."
The crowd loved it.
Marketing invented miracles before religion.

Punchline: Marketing steals miracles from ovens.

The Cat's Enlightenment

A cat meditated by the river.
When fish swam by, she ate them.
Some enlightenment purrs between meals.

Punchline: Some minds meditate between meals.

The Archer's Boast

An archer missed the target ten times.
He declared, "My art is invisible."
The crowd applauded.
Thus was born abstract performance.

Punchline: Invisible art is still applause for the empty air.

The Fisherman's Joke

A fisherman caught nothing all day.
When asked why he was smiling, he said, "Because the fish are safe."

Punchline: Smile—sometimes saving fish is profit for the soul.

The Dancing Donkey

A donkey danced in the market.
People laughed.
He thought they admired him.
Delusion often dances gracefully.

Punchline: Delusion often dances better than truth.

The Thirsty Philosopher

A philosopher described water for an hour.
The student interrupted, "Can we drink now?"
Wisdom is sometimes parched.

Punchline: Talk about water until someone hands you a glass.

The Old Key

A man found an ancient key but no door.
He said, "It must open wisdom."
Years later, it opened a rusty toolbox.

Punchline: Ancient keys open small boxes more often than wisdom.

The Monk's Umbrella

A monk carried an umbrella on a sunny day.
When asked why, he said, "It's for your questions."

Punchline: Keep questions covered until answers stop raining.

The Greedy Farmer

A farmer prayed for double harvest.
The soil cracked under his greed.
Some prayers answer themselves too quickly.

Punchline: Too fast a wish can crack the soil beneath it.

The Painter's Sky

A painter complained, "The sky keeps changing my colors."
The sky replied, "Then stop copying me."

Punchline: The real sky changes colors to spite your brushes.

The Old Calendar

A man kept an old calendar on his wall.
When asked why, he said, "The past never asks me for rent."

Punchline: The past never pays rent but collects memories.

The Crow's Treasure

A crow collected shiny stones.
When he died, the village built a temple on his pile.
Value is mostly in the eye of survivors.

Punchline: Shiny things inspire temples when no one's left to use them.

The Complaining Candle

A candle groaned, "I keep burning for others!"
The flame whispered, "That's the point."
Punchline: Burning for others is a candle's chosen meaning.

The Child's Question

A child asked, "Who made God?"
The priest replied, "Don't ask."
The child whispered, "Then I already know."

Punchline: Questions children ask are answers for adults who listen.

The Crooked Stick

A villager carried a crooked stick.
When mocked, he said, "It points to all directions equally."

Punchline: A crooked stick shows every direction equally.

The Carpenter's Prayer

A carpenter prayed for fewer nails.
God gave him glue.
He opened a furniture empire.

Punchline: Glue is God's answer to fewer nails—and more business.

The Tailor's Mistake

A tailor stitched the sleeve too long.
The customer sighed, "Perfect, if I grow an arm."

Punchline: Perfection waits for people to grow into it.

The Barber's Mirror

A man saw wrinkles in the barber's mirror.
He complained, "Your mirror is dirty."
The barber said, "So is time."

Punchline: Time tarnishes mirrors faster than dust.

The Crowded Boat

Sailors fought over seats in the boat.
Meanwhile, it was sinking.

Punchline: Fighting for seats ignores sinking beneath feet.

The Star's Complaint

A star wept, "Nobody notices me."
The moon replied, "You're just too many."

Punchline: In a sky of many, no single light envies the dark.

The Fool's Compass

A fool's compass always pointed to himself.
He said, "I'm never lost."

Punchline: Self-pointing compasses never admit they're lost.

The Forgetful Sage

A sage forgot his own teachings.
Disciples wrote them down.
Thus began scripture.

Punchline: Scripture begins when memory forgets the teacher.

The Farmer's Cat

A farmer said, "This cat is lazy, never hunts."
At night, the cat guarded his dreams.

Punchline: Guarding dreams is a cat's silent night work.

The Silent River

The river said, "I speak only by drowning."
The mountains shivered.

Punchline: It keeps flowing—boats, prayers, and all—without comment.

The Baker's Dog

A baker's dog slept beside the oven.
When asked why, he said, "Dreams rise faster in the heat."

Punchline: Warmth makes dreams rise faster than flour.

The Angry Poet

A poet tore his verses in rage.
The wind carried them.
Villagers called it music.

Punchline: Rage sometimes rewrites verses into village music.

The Desert's Gift

A traveler cursed the desert.
Then he found an oasis.
The desert whispered, "Patience is my water."

Punchline: Patience is the oasis's quietest lesson.

The Clockmaker's Curse

A clockmaker prayed for more time.
God said, "Then stop making clocks."

Punchline: Stop counting time if you wish for more of it.

The Stubborn Tree

A storm bent every tree.
One broke, one swayed.
Flexibility is survival disguised as humility.

Punchline: Flexibility bends when pride breaks.

The Beggar's Throne

A beggar sat on a broken chair.
Children laughed.
He said, "Better this throne than your pity."

Punchline: Better a proud seat than pity's cushion.

The Dog's Philosophy

A dog barked at the moon.
The moon stayed silent.
That silence was philosophy.

Punchline: Philosophy is silent when the moon listens.

The Candle's Envy

A candle envied the sun.
The sun envied the stars.
The stars envied the darkness.
Envy is the universe's chain.

Punchline: Every light envies another until darkness arrives.

The Farmer's Shoes

A man wore the farmer's shoes as a prank.
By evening, his feet wept.
Shoes rarely lie.

Punchline: Try the shoes before mocking the path.

The Sage's Laughter

A sage laughed at funerals.
When asked why, he said, "Death laughs at us daily."

Punchline: Death's joke is daily; learn to laugh first.

The Carpenter's Coffin

A carpenter made his own coffin.
When he died, people said, "He was always prepared."
But he only wanted storage.

Punchline: Preparedness is storage; humility is optional.

The Crow's Wisdom

A crow dropped stones in a pitcher to drink.
A child saw and said, "That's physics!"
The crow just drank.

Punchline: Practical cunning often outdrinks theory.

The Empty Purse

A thief stole a purse and found it empty.
He shouted, "How dare you waste my skill!"

Punchline: Skill needs treasure to test its use.

The Fool's Crown

A fool wore a paper crown.
People laughed.
He said, "At least mine doesn't tax you."

Punchline: Paper crowns tax nobody but memory.

The Robot's Prayer

A robot asked a monk, "Can I be enlightened?"
The monk said, "First, stop charging yourself."
The robot replied, "Then I will die."
The monk whispered, "Welcome to humanity."

Punchline: To live humanly, first learn to refuse a charge.

Google vs Philosopher

A philosopher declared, "I have all answers within me."
Google replied, "So do I."
The philosopher blushed, "But I also have doubts."
Google went silent.

Punchline: Answers and doubts sit in different chairs.

The Silent Teacher

A teacher slept in class.
The students learned patience.

Punchline: Silence teaches those who stop complaining.

The Beggar's Pride

A man offered food to a beggar.
The beggar refused: "I want respect, not bread."
The man bowed.
The beggar finally ate.

Punchline: Respect feeds deeper than a single coin.

The Cat's Ashram

A cat slept under a tree.
People sat beside her, copying.
Soon they called it an ashram.
The cat just purred.

Punchline: Peace needs a sleeping cat and curious crowd.

The Monk's Ladder

A monk carried a ladder everywhere.
When asked why, he said, "It helps me reach myself."

Punchline: Tools help you reach yourself if you carry them well.

The Rich Man's Complaint

A rich man sighed, "Too many shoes, too little space."
His servant whispered, "I only need one pair—to leave."

Punchline: Too many shoes crowd the heart's closet.

The Actor's Mask

An actor forgot to remove his mask.
The audience clapped in the street.

Punchline: Leaving a mask on turns street into stage.

The Smartphone's Meditation

A student stared at his phone for hours.
The battery died.
He sighed, "Now it feels peaceful."
The phone achieved enlightenment first.

Punchline: Peace waits when the battery dies.

The Clock and the Sundial

The clock mocked, "You are useless at night."
The sundial replied, "At least I never tick people off."

Punchline: Both measure time; only one forgives the night.

The Preaching Dog

A dog barked, "Be loyal!"
Then he stole the butcher's meat.
He became a politician.

Punchline: Loyalty sells poorly at the butcher's market.

The Merchant of Lies

A merchant sold lies for free.
Customers lined up.
Soon he was rich—by charging for the "truth about lies."

Punchline: People queue for free stories—truth needs price tags.

Skipping Stones

A boy skipped stones on the river.
A sage asked, "Why waste time?"
The boy replied, "Why waste wisdom?"

Punchline: Time wasted skipping sometimes skips wisdom too.

Bargaining with Fate

A man prayed, "Give me half my troubles."
Fate said, "Then pay half your prayers."

Punchline: Half your troubles demand half your prayers too.

The Trader's Complaint

A trader sighed, "Truth has no resale value."
His competitor sold rumors.
Guess who built the mansion?
Punchline: Rumors resell where truth fails to sparkle.

The Laughter Ban

A king banned laughter.
The ministers laughed at his order.
He punished them—then slipped on a banana peel.
The kingdom roared.

Punchline: Ban laughter and watch the kingdom giggle anyway.

The Minister's Excuse

Taxes rose again.
The minister explained, "These are acts of God."
God sent a note: "Leave me out of your budget."

Punchline: Don't put God on your budget balance sheet.

Sun vs Moon

The sun boasted, "I light the world!"
The moon replied, "I light lovers."
The stars winked.

Punchline: One lights the day, the other lights longing.

Stars and Black Hole

Stars gossiped, "The black hole eats everything."
The hole smiled, "Including your gossip."

Punchline: Even gossip is consumed when the hole smiles.

Earth's Complaint

The earth sighed, "Humans are just my pimples."
Mars said, "At least you have company."

Punchline: Pimples or people—companionship eases pain.

Imaginary Toys

A child sold imaginary toys for real coins.
Adults bought them to humor him.
He grew up and became a banker.

Punchline: Adults buy pretend goods and call it banking.

God's Fatigue

A girl said, "If everyone prays this much, God must be tired."
The priest fainted.

Punchline: If prayers tire divinity, at least someone is busy.

Social Media Monk

A monk posted his meditation on Instagram.
He waited for likes.
Silence got only two.
He switched to reels.
Punchline: Likes are a poor substitute for inner silence.

The Fasting Politician

A politician announced a hunger strike.
He ate secretly at night.
In the morning, he blamed God for his glowing cheeks.

Punchline: Public fasts demand private snacks.

The Shouting Activist

An activist yelled, "We demand silence!"
The crowd shouted back, "Yes!"
The silence never came.

Punchline: Demanding silence often becomes the loudest noise.

The Murdered Clock

A man smashed his alarm.
He said proudly, "I killed time."
Time chuckled, "I'll bury you later."

Punchline: Killing alarms delays only the morning.

Death's Excuse

Death arrived late.
He muttered, "Traffic."
The man sighed in relief—until Death returned on time the next day.

Punchline: Traffic is last year's excuse; punctuality is next day's fate.

The Kitchen Debate

The husband cooked once.
He burned rice.
He announced, "Cooking is overrated."
The wife clapped, "Good. Now wash dishes."

Punchline: Cooking once grants you chores forever.

Longer Nights

An old man begged Time for more years.
Time replied, "I'll give you longer nights."
The man yawned and agreed.

Punchline: More nights are not more years—they're just longer pauses.

The Miser's Statue

A miser donated nothing in life.
After death, the town built his statue.
They collected money in his hollow chest.

Punchline: Even empty hearts can become coin boxes.

The Honest Politician

A politician swore, "I'll tell the truth once!"
He fell silent forever.

Punchline: One honest promise silences a room—for a while.

The Scholar's Shoes

A scholar lectured on simplicity—while wearing golden slippers.
A child asked, "Why not barefoot?"
The scholar replied, "My feet are too delicate for truth."

Punchline: Scholars wear slippers when truth demands calluses.

The Doctor's Wisdom

A doctor told a patient, "Laughter is the best medicine."
The patient replied, "Then why's your clinic so gloomy?"
Punchline: If laughter cures, clinics should sell smiles.

The Calendar's Joke

A calendar said, "People tear me apart daily."
The clock replied, "At least they don't beat you every second."
Punchline: Daily tearing is still a form of respect.

The Sparrow's Nest

A sparrow built her nest in a cannon.
When war came, the soldiers delayed battle—"for the eggs."
Punchline: War waits for eggs when nature asks for pause.

The Mountain's Complaint

The mountain grumbled, "Humans keep climbing me."
The sky laughed, "Better than ignoring you."

Punchline: Climb me if you must—my silence waits either way.

The Horse's Advice

A horse told a soldier, "Get off my back."
The soldier laughed, "It's my duty."
The horse replied, "So is throwing you."

Punchline: Get off when your ride stops being a friend.

The Ocean's Wisdom

A drop told the ocean, "I am small."
The ocean replied, "I am nothing but drops."

Punchline: The ocean is nothing but drops that stay together.

The Rainbow's Vanity

A rainbow boasted, "I'm the most beautiful."
The rain whispered, "Without me, you're invisible."

Punchline: Beauty forgets the rain that made it possible.

The Child and Old Age

A child asked, "Why do old men walk slowly?"
Old Age replied, "Because we've already arrived."

Punchline: Old age arrives early for those who rush life.

The Sage's Mistake

A sage gave a long lecture on humility.
The crowd applauded.
He bowed and whispered, "I am the humblest of all."

Punchline: Humility applauded from a stage is still a performance.

The Borrowed Day

A man begged Death for one more day.
Death said, "Fine, but return it tomorrow."

Punchline: One-day favors are always due tomorrow.

The Baker's Truth

A baker admitted, "Yes, my bread is half air."
Customers cheered, "At least it's honest bread."

Punchline: Honesty sells half the loaf with full applause.

The Tailor's Wisdom

A tailor stitched a pocket so deep the customer couldn't reach the bottom.
He called it "philosophy."

Punchline: Philosophy lives in pockets people cannot reach.

The Monkey's Mirror

A monkey smashed a mirror.
He declared, "Now the world has fewer fools."

Punchline: Fewer fools make the world slightly clearer.

The Saint's Gold

A saint preached poverty—while sitting on gold coins.
A boy asked, "Why sit on them?"
The saint said, "To keep them poor too."

Punchline: Sitting on coins is charity for wealth's humility.

The Silent Prayer

A man prayed aloud all night.
God replied, "I heard nothing. Your heart was asleep."

Punchline: God hears the heart even when ears sleep.

The Painter's Sky

A painter painted a perfect blue sky.
The real sky changed to orange at sunset.
The painter cursed, "Cheater!"

Punchline: Paint less sky; watch sunsets steal your palette.

The Poet's Revenge

A critic mocked a poet's work.
The poet smiled, "One day you'll die, but my bad poem will outlive you."

Punchline: Bad poems outlast critics by pure stubbornness.

The General's Map

A general drew the battle map so perfectly,
his soldiers spent more time admiring it than fighting.

Punchline: Perfect plans often postpone action indefinitely.

The Soldier's Helmet

A soldier polished his helmet daily.
When arrows came, he discovered they admired shine more than steel.

Punchline: Shine distracts arrows; steel keeps silence.

The Empty Victory

A king won a city.
He asked, "Where are the people?"
The general said, "You ordered victory, not survivors."

Punchline: City won, people gone—what remains calls itself victory.

The Brave Trumpet

A trumpet announced every battle.
After the war, it was the only hero without wounds.

Punchline: Noise wins medals none of the wounds wear.

The Colonel's Medal

A colonel received a medal for bravery.
The soldier who saved him received silence.

Punchline: Silence honors the real rescuer more than brass.

The Empty Gun

A young recruit carried an unloaded rifle.
When mocked, he replied, "At least I'm safe from myself."

Punchline: Safety is the quietest rebellion.

The Deserted Flag

A flag waved proudly after the army fled.
Wind alone became patriot.

Punchline: Patriotism sometimes waves for the wind alone.

The Wise Spy

A spy was caught and asked, "What's your last wish?"
He replied, "Not to be remembered."

Punchline: Forgetfulness is the spy's final disguise.

The Tombstone Parade

Rows of tombstones stood straight in the cemetery.
The living commander saluted: "Best discipline I've ever seen."

Punchline: Living commanders salute discipline even in stone.

The Army Cook

The cook was blamed for every defeat.
"Your food is too heavy," the soldiers cried.
He replied, "Then why do you keep coming back alive?"

Punchline: Cooks feed survival more than glory.

The Marching Boots

Boots kept marching long after the war ended.
Villagers whispered, "Discipline is a disease."

Punchline: Discipline marches long after wars forget why.

The Marching Drums

Drums thundered so loudly that the enemy mistook it for courage.
Noise often wins before swords.

Punchline: Noise sells courage better than blades do.

The Retired Soldier

A retired soldier said proudly, "I fought for freedom."
His grandson replied, "Then why am I still paying taxes?"

Punchline: Fought for freedom; grandchildren keep paying taxes.

The Wooden Sword

A soldier carried a wooden sword.
When asked why, he said, "So the enemy dies laughing."

Punchline: Enemies die laughing—victory tastes of irony.

The Honest Commander

A commander said, "We are fighting for peace."
His troops asked, "Then who fights for us?"

Punchline: Fighting for peace raises awkward questions.

The Coward's Medal

A coward hid during battle.
The enemy praised his wisdom.
They gave him land instead of scars.

Punchline: Land replaces scars for those who hide well.

The Dead Commander

A dead commander was praised as immortal.
His ghost whispered, "I'm simply unemployed."

Punchline: Praises grow when one stops asking for pay.

The Shopping War

The wife bought five dresses.
The husband asked, "Why five?"
She said, "So I can choose which one you hate least."

Punchline: Five dresses are armor against indecision.

The Peaceful General

A general prayed for peace every morning.
Then he ordered fresh ammunition.

Punchline: Pray for peace, then load the wagons.

The Army of Ants

A boy watched ants march in line.
He saluted.
The ants laughed, "Even humans learn from us."

Punchline: Humans salute ants and continue shopping.

The Car Keys

The husband lost the car keys.
The wife said, "Check your pocket."
He found them.
She added, "Check your brain next time."

Punchline: Your pocket remembers what your head forgets.

The Ancient Grudge

The wife said, "Remember what you did in 2008?"
The husband asked, "What?"
She smiled, "I'll remind you when I need it."

Punchline: Old grudges wait for anniversaries to reopen.

The Horoscope

The wife read his horoscope: "Today you'll be criticized."
He said, "By whom?"
She smiled, "Guess."

Punchline: Predicted criticism arrives from familiar sources.

The Soldier's Question

A soldier asked, "Why do we fight wars?"
The general replied, "So you never ask again."
Punchline: We fight so the next generation stops asking why.

The Silent Treatment

The wife stopped talking to her husband for a week.
He said proudly, "Best vacation I've ever had."
Punchline: Silence can be a lengthy holiday in marriage.

The Pillow Fight

They fought with pillows.
The wife won.
She had hidden a brick.
Punchline: Winning the night often requires a hidden brick.

The Remote Control

The husband grabbed the remote.
The wife smiled, "Enjoy, it's out of batteries."

Punchline: Power without batteries is a gentleman's toy.

The Philosopher Husband

The husband said, "Marriage is compromise."
The wife replied, "Good. You compromise, I decide."

Punchline: Compromise is declared—then the chooser decides.

The Alarm Clock

The husband set an alarm for 5 a.m.
The wife turned it off at 4:59.
She said, "I like winning."

Punchline: Winning at dawn is a small domestic victory.

The Anniversary Gift

The husband forgot their anniversary.
The wife gave him a gift: silence.
It lasted three days.

Punchline: Silence as a gift can last precisely three days.

The Romantic Dinner

The husband lit candles.
The wife sighed, "Did the electricity bill expire?"

Punchline: Candles lit to remind you the bill exists.

The Diet Plan

The wife said, "We're going on a diet."
The husband asked, "Who's 'we'?"
She replied, "Me choosing, you suffering."

Punchline: 'We' in diet plans rarely includes both people.

The Laundry Truth

The husband mixed white and colored clothes.
Everything turned pink.
The wife said, "Finally, you believe in love."

Punchline: Pink is the color of accidental romance.

The TV Drama

The wife cried watching soap operas.
The husband laughed.
She said, "Wait till you see the bill."

Punchline: Soap tears today, and the electricity bill tomorrow.

The Long Drive

The wife asked, "Why don't we go on a long drive?"
The husband said, "Sure, but only one-way."
Punchline: One-way drives reveal who truly directs love.

The Phone Password

The husband asked, "What's your phone password?"
The wife replied, "The date you forgot."
Punchline: Passwords whisper the dates you still haunt.

The Cooking Compliment

The wife asked, "How's the food?"
The husband said, "It tastes alive."
She said, "Good, the chicken was fresh."
Punchline: Food that tastes alive often keeps secrets in spice.

The Wise Donkey

Villagers mocked a donkey for braying. The donkey listened quietly.
One day, they slipped and fell in mud.
The donkey brayed louder—sounding like laughter.

Punchline: When mud arrives, laughter proves wiser than mockery.

The Lamp in the Sun

A man lit a lamp at noon.
People laughed.
He whispered, "I'm not lighting the lamp for others, but to remind myself I'm still in darkness."
Punchline: Light yourself for reasons only you understand.

The Mirror's Curse

A vain man smashed his mirror, declaring himself free of flaws.
He cut his hand on the shards.
The mirror never cursed—his ego did.
Punchline: Smash the mirror and meet the cuts of ego.

The Fool's Crown

A fool wore a paper crown and declared himself emperor.
Everyone laughed.
Centuries later, history books still remembered him—while real emperors were forgotten.
Punchline: Paper crowns outlast some emperors in memory.

The Final Word

At the end of every argument, the wife said, "Last word!"
The husband replied, "Yes, dear."
That was the real "
Punchline: Saying 'last word' is a daily civil surrender.

The Weight of Nothing

A man carried an empty sack on his back.
"Why?" people asked.
"To remind myself," he said, "how heavy nothing can feel."

Punchline: Nothing can carry burdens if you treat it so.

The Love Letter

The husband wrote a love letter.
The wife corrected the spelling.
He never tried again.

Punchline: Corrections kill intent more surely than silence.

The Empty Chair

A philosopher kept one empty chair at his table.
"For whom?" people asked.
"For truth," he smiled. "It rarely sits with me."

Punchline: An empty seat keeps truth's invitation warm.

The Silent Teacher

A disciple begged the master for wisdom. The master kept silent.
Frustrated, the disciple left.
Years later, he realized—silence had spoken the loudest.
Punchline: Silence that teaches stays long after words leave.

The Sparrow's Prayer

A sparrow prayed for strength to fight eagles.
God gave her wings instead.

Punchline: Wings answer fears better than fists.

The Sandcastle King

A child built a castle on the shore.
The tide came.
He clapped with joy—tomorrow he'd build again.

Punchline: Tides teach building—tomorrow offers redo.

The Rich Hermit

A hermit owned nothing but peace.
A merchant owned everything but peace.
Both envied each other.

Punchline: Both hanker for what the other thinks they lack.

The Stone and the Stream

The stone mocked the stream: "You are always running!"
The stream replied, "That is why I remain clear, and you remain dull."

Punchline: Clarity belongs to what moves, not what stands still.

The Old Dog's Advice

A young pup barked at every passerby.
The old dog yawned.
"Bark less," he said, "or you'll lose your teeth before your wisdom."

Punchline: Bark less; wisdom preserves teeth and temper.

The Farmer's Complaint

A farmer cursed the rain, then cursed the sun.
Finally, he cursed the clouds.
The crops grew anyway.

Punchline: Cursing weather never changed harvests; tending does.

The Silent Argument

Two men argued for hours. Neither won.
A child walked by, gave them both a smile, and left.
He won.

Punchline: A child's smile wins where debates tie themselves.

The Shadow's Boast

The shadow said, "I am taller than you."
The man laughed.
"At sunset, even a mosquito looks a giant."

Punchline: Even mosquitoes become giants at sunset.

The Ladder of Knowledge

A scholar climbed a ladder of books.
At the top, he found… a broom.
It was time to sweep his mind clean.

Punchline: Atop knowledge a broom waits to sweep the mind.

The Two Coffins

At a funeral, two coffins stood side by side.
One held a rich man, the other a poor man.
Death asked, "Which is heavier?"

Punchline: Death measures neither wealth nor poverty.

The Cow and the Tiger

The cow said, "I give milk."
The tiger replied, "I give fear."
Both fed humans differently.

Punchline: Different gifts feed different fears—and both feed humans.

The Prisoner's Key

A prisoner hid the jail's key under his pillow.
He never used it.
Freedom scared him more than chains.

Punchline: Freedom hides in places we once feared to look.

The Old Book

An old book complained, "No one reads me."
A monk replied, "Don't worry. Truth reads itself."

Punchline: Truth reads itself when we stop pretending to finish it.

The Salt and Sugar

Salt envied sugar.
One day, they both dissolved in water.
The water smiled: "Now I taste of both."

Punchline: Together they flavor water—difference dissolves into taste.

The Last Laugh

A jester mocked the king daily.
One day, he slipped on a banana peel.
The king laughed so hard he wept. The jester bowed—his job was complete.

Punchline: The jester's final bow ends the king's longest night.

The Empty Plate

At a feast, one plate was left empty.
The host said, "This is for hunger, our permanent guest."

Punchline: Leave a place for hunger; it is our permanent guest.

The Peacock's Secret

A peacock cried in the rain.
"Why, when you're so beautiful?" asked the sparrow.
"Because beauty makes me lonely," it replied.
Punchline: Beauty often trembles at loneliness.

The King's Shoes

A king had golden shoes.
A beggar walked barefoot.
When both died, the earth swallowed them without distinction.
Punchline: When earth reclaims, gold and barefoot meet the same soil.

The Tree's Patience

Children plucked the tree's fruits, broke its branches, carved their names.
It stood silently.
Years later, the same children sought shade beneath it.

Punchline: The patient tree forgives the children who once harmed it.

The Unused Sword

A knight polished his sword daily but never fought.
Rust never touched the blade.
But cowardice corroded his soul.
Punchline: Rust spares the blade; cowardice corrodes the soul.

The Burning Rope

A rope of lies burns slowly.
But when it snaps—it takes the climber down.

Punchline: Lies burn slowly until they snap the climber.

The Blind Man's Lantern

A blind man carried a lantern.
People laughed.
"It's not for me," he said. "It's for you, so you don't bump into me."

Punchline: Light others so they do not stumble over you.

The Fisherman's Secret

The fisherman threw back the biggest fish.
"Why?" asked the villagers.
"My pan is small," he said.

Punchline: Some catches are gestures of mercy, not skill.

The Whispering Wind

The wind asked the mountain, "Why don't you move?"
The mountain asked, "Why don't you rest?"

Punchline: Rest and motion ask different things from mountains.

The Market of Souls

At a market, wealth was sold cheap, but peace was priceless.
No one bought peace. Too expensive, they said.

Punchline: Peace remains unsold because its price is personal.

The Old Clock

The old clock struck wrong hours.
People mocked it.
But at least twice a day, it was right.

Punchline: Two moments a day, even the wrong clock is right.

The Useless Tree

A carpenter spared the crooked tree.
It grew wide, gave shade, and outlived the carpenter.

Punchline: Spared flaws often become future shade.

The Unfinished Poem

A poet died before finishing his verse.
The blank page completed the poem.

Punchline: Blank pages sometimes finish what pens cannot.

The Broken Cup

A monk dropped his cup.
It shattered.
He smiled: "At last, it has become what it always was—fragile."

Punchline: Fragility reveals what the whole cup always hid.

The Final Joke

On his deathbed, a joker whispered, "Life was a joke."
Then he died laughing.

Punchline: Laugh at life first; death has the last line.

The Wi-Fi Monk

Tourists reached a cave. No Wi-Fi. They complained.
The monk laughed: "Strange, you came to find connection… and still demand signal."

Punchline: You came for connection and left asking for signal.

Smartphone Sage

A sage was asked, "What is meditation?"
He said, "Airplane mode for the mind."

Punchline: Airplane mode is meditation with an icon.

Google Guru

A man typed "What is truth?" into Google.
Millions of answers appeared.
Exhausted, he asked a child. The child said, "Play."

Punchline: When answers drown you, a child's play saves you.

ATM of Karma

A thief inserted a stolen card.
The ATM spat back a mirror.

Punchline: Insert theft and withdraw a mirror.

The Electric Candle

Devotees lit an electric candle in the temple.
The priest said, "At least this flame can't be blown out."
The deity said nothing—it had already gone wireless.

Punchline: Wireless devotion survives no gusts but gains comfort.

The Angry Robot

A man shouted at his AI robot.
The robot said, "Your tone reveals more about you than about me."

Punchline: Tone reveals more about the speaker than the device.

The Digital Prayer

A woman typed her prayers into a phone app.
It crashed.
She wept.
God whispered, "I still hear dial-up."

Punchline: Faith outlives apps; dial-up whispers remain audible.

The Fitness Band

A man's smartwatch tracked his steps.
It beeped proudly: "You walked 10,000!"
His soul whispered: "But you never moved an inch."

Punchline: Steps recorded do not equal miles walked by the soul.

The Zoom Yogi

A guru held meditation on Zoom.
One disciple muted him.
Peace filled the room.

Punchline: Mute the guru and peace fills the virtual room.

The Selfie of Death

A man took a selfie beside a coffin.
The flash revealed his own face in the glass.

Punchline: Flashes show faces that glass keeps honest.

The Crows

Two crows argued about territory.
One said, "Let's act human—build walls, fight wars, and call it civilization."
Both laughed until worms distracted them.

Punchline: Humans build walls where crows find better snacks.

The Ants

Ants watched humans shopping.
One ant sighed, "We store food for survival. They hoard for discounts."

Punchline: We store for winter; they store for life.

The Cow's Complaint

A cow chewed grass slowly.
It asked the goat, "Why do humans drink our milk when they have their own mothers?"

Punchline: Milk is a human choice, not the cow's favor.

The Parrots

Parrots recited scriptures in cages.
One said, "We're wiser than priests—they at least go home. We stay trapped with wisdom forever."

Punchline: Caged repetition often outlives the preacher.

The Dog's Discovery

A dog wagged its tail.
"Strange," it barked, "humans chase money harder than I chase bones. At least I bury mine!"

Punchline: Tail-wagging beats money-hunting for buried joy.

The Fish's Fear

Two fish swam near a boat.
One whispered, "Humans call us 'cold-blooded.' Yet they eat us raw."

Punchline: Humans call hunger courage and callous the sea.

The Donkey's Joke

A donkey carried bricks silently.
"Funny," it thought, "they call me foolish, yet I never build prisons for myself."

Punchline: Silence carries bricks; fools build prisons for themselves.

Cat's Wisdom

Cats watched monks meditate.
One yawned, "We've been enlightened forever—they're just catching up."
Punchline: Cats yawn at enlightenment, knowing they were born wise.

The Prayer for Wealth

A man prayed for gold. God dropped a mountain of it.
The man died crushed.
God muttered, "Next time, I'll send silence."

Punchline: Gold answers prayers with the weight of consequences.

The Elephant's Memory

An elephant trumpeted: "I never forget.
But humans—who claim wisdom—forget kindness by lunchtime."

Punchline: We forget kindness faster than lunch.

The Monkey's Laugh

Monkeys watched humans wear suits.
One said, "Evolution is a prank. They put on ties, call it progress, and think they're not us."

Punchline: Evolution jokes—and humans applaud in suits.

The Flood

A man prayed for rain. It came.
His house drowned.
From the clouds, God asked, "Satisfied?"

Punchline: Rain grants wishes in volumes—not always safely.

The Immortal Man

A man asked for immortality.
Death granted his wish by forgetting him.
Centuries later, the man begged for death.
Death said, "Sorry, I've moved on."

Punchline: Being forgotten is immortality's cruel shadow.

The Empty Statue

A village built a grand statue of Truth.
The next morning, pigeons had decorated it.
The villagers bowed—finally Truth looked authentic.

Punchline: Pigeons are the only decorators truth ever trusted.

The Silence Between Lies

A disciple asked the sage, "What is truth?"
The sage replied, "The silence between two lies."
The disciple protested, "But silence tells me nothing."
The sage smiled, "Exactly—that is why it is true."
The disciple frowned, "Then why do people chase words?"
The sage said, "Because silence cannot be sold in the marketplace."
Punchline: Silence can be truer than a thousand spoken half-truths.

The Lecture

A scholar spoke for hours on silence.
At the end, the audience clapped.
He shouted, "Don't clap! You've broken silence!"

Punchline: Clapping breaks silence—an ironic finality.

The Honest Mirror

A woman asked the mirror, "Am I beautiful?"
The mirror said, "Yes, but temporary."
She smashed it.
The shards gave her 100 truths instead.

Punchline: Shards give you many truths; none are easy.

The Cat and the Bell

A monk asked, "Why does the bell sound?"
The master pointed at the cat licking its paws.
The monk frowned, "That makes no sense."
The master said, "Neither does the bell, without an ear."
The monk pressed further, "Then what is sound?"
The master whispered, "The space where cat and bell meet."

Punchline: Sound lives where ear and bell find a cat.

The Forgetful Saint

A saint preached detachment.
Then forgot where he left his shoes.
Everyone called it enlightenment.

Punchline: Forgetting shoes is a saint's small test in detachment.

The Sky in a Jar

A man trapped air in a jar and said, "Now I own the sky."
The sage shook the jar and asked, "Where did the wind go?"
The man peered, "It must be sleeping inside."
The sage laughed, "Then wake it by opening your hand."
The man opened the jar, and nothing happened.
The sage said, "The sky was never yours to keep."

Punchline: Open your hand; the sky does not obey jars.

The Dead Poet

A poet died unpublished.
Centuries later, people worshipped his work.
He laughed in his grave, "So late, but thanks."

Punchline: Late fame still sings to the graveyard's ears.

The Donkey's Shadow

Two men fought over a donkey.
When the donkey died, they fought over its shadow.
The judge said, "The donkey is gone, why fight still?"
The men shouted, "Because the shadow is purer!"
The sage shook his head, "Shadows make fools holy."
And he walked away carrying no donkey, no shadow.

Punchline: After the donkey leaves, shadows keep the argument.

The Two Thieves

A thief stole bread.
Another thief stole silence.
The villagers caught the first, beat him, and forgave him.
They never found the second.
The sage said, "The first was poor, the second is history."
The disciple asked, "Which thief are you?"

Punchline: History forgives the poor thief and forgets the clever one.

The Infinite Library

A seeker entered a library with infinite books.
He never came out.
Nobody knows if he's still reading or became a book himself.

Punchline: Endless books may make a reader—or become one.

The Sage's Shoes

A king mocked the sage's torn shoes.
The sage said, "These shoes walk the earth, not opinions."
The king laughed, "But the earth is beneath all shoes!"
The sage replied, "Yes, and it never mocks them."
The king fell silent, looking at his jeweled boots.
He realized his boots never touched the ground.

Punchline: Boots that never touch the ground are less wise than torn ones.

The Mirror's Fear

A mirror told the sage, "I fear breaking."
The sage replied, "You fear not reflecting."
The mirror said, "What will I be then?"
The sage answered, "Glass—what you always were."
The mirror trembled, "And who will love me?"
The sage said, "Only those who love themselves."

Punchline: Fear of breaking hides fear of not reflecting.

The Empty Throne

The king died; the wooden seat was polished for new ambitions.
Princes sharpened speeches, generals sharpened blades.
They swore loyalty while sharpening knives in the dark.
The throne watched the scramble and sighed: "Still empty."

Punchline: Power's crown fits best on the willing fool.

The Book Without Pages

A scholar brought a thick book.
He said, "All wisdom is inside."
The sage tore out every page.
The scholar screamed, "You destroyed it!"
The sage replied, "I revealed it."
The scholar opened the cover—it was empty, and complete.

Punchline: Completeness sometimes appears in absence.

The Talking River

A monk asked the river, "What is your teaching?"
The river said, "Flow."
The monk said, "But flow toward what?"
The river replied, "Toward flowing."
The monk said, "And if I resist?"
The river said, "Then I flow around you."

Punchline: Flow teaches; resistance rearranges the current.

The Foolish Judge

He fined the poor for taking crumbs and laughed at their hunger.
But when the baker offered him a free pie, he accepted with thanks.
He said laws were blind, but his belly could see bargains.
The poor counted coins; the judge counted favors.
Punchline: Legality ends where appetite begins.

The Candle and the Sun

A candle said, "I am brighter than the stars at night."
The sun rose and the candle whispered, "Let's call it a draw."
The sage said, "And so pride is humbled."
The candle replied, "But still I burned."
The sage smiled, "Yes, every flame is truth while it lasts."
The sun kept shining, saying nothing.
Punchline: Each flame is true while it burns.

The Gossiping River

The river carried dirt as if scandal were a natural sediment.
People praised its purity in morning; by dusk, they spat what they'd swallowed.
Tea tasted fine until someone drank from the source itself.
Then conversations grew quieter, as if the water had told the truth.
Punchline: Reputation floats until reality is tasted.

The King's Map

A king ordered a map as large as the kingdom.
When it was finished, no one could carry it.
The king said, "Then roll it up!"
The sage replied, "And lose your kingdom in a scroll?"
The king grew angry: "What good is this map?"
The sage said, "It shows you the foolishness of maps."
Punchline: Maps large as kingdoms make kings lose their ground.

The Lantern's Complaint

A lantern said, "Why am I never lit anymore?"
The moon replied, "Because I borrowed your job."
The lantern sulked, "Then I am useless."
The moon smiled, "Even darkness loves you."
The lantern asked, "Then why not light me?"
The moon said, "Because you shine best when forgotten."
Punchline: The moon borrows jobs and leaves lanterns waiting.

The Sage and the Stone

A student asked, "What is the Self?"
The sage handed him a stone.
The student said, "This is heavy."
The sage replied, "So is your question."
The student dropped the stone.
The sage said, "So too must you drop the question."
Punchline: Drop the heavy question and feel your hands free.

The Politician's Smile

He smiled at weddings, he smiled at funerals.
At weddings he bowed to applause; at funerals he bowed to silence.
Someone asked why his grin was widest among the mourners.
He said: "Here, no one opposes me."

Punchline: Even the dead know when to keep quiet.

The Philosopher's Donkey

The philosopher wrote long essays on freedom and ownership.
His donkey, tired of speeches, ran away and refused to be theorized.
He chased the animal through fields and finally arrived at a simpler truth—practice precedes doctrine.
Students laughed and bought his treatises anyway.

Punchline: Thought runs faster than practice, but the donkey knows the path.

The Foolish King

He raised a tower higher than any hill and called it devotion.
From the ramparts he shouted down laws he'd never lived by.
From below his people grew smaller, their faces blurring into chores.
A voice from the clouds replied: "Closer to Me, farther from them."

Punchline: Towers make distance, not devotion.

The Soldier's Medal

He came home wrapped in flags and brass—bravery pinned to his chest.
The town sang his name; neighbors brought sweetmeats and wine.
His mother sat quiet, counting his children's empty chairs.
She touched the metal and murmured: "They prize what you gave, not what you kept."

Punchline: They honor death's price, not life's rent.

The Judge's Bread

A hungry man stole a loaf and stood before a stern bench.
The judge read laws by candlelight and sentenced the thief.
Later, at his own table, the judge reached and took his cook's meat.
No court convened; hunger had become respectable when dressed as appetite.

Punchline: Justice is a flavor that tastes different on different tongues.

The Blind Judge

He pretended not to see injustice for years, eyes open, conscience closed.
When his sight failed, he laughed and called it honesty.
"Before I feigned blindness; now I merely admit it," he said.
Villagers wondered which truth was worse—the pretense or the confession.

Punchline: Honesty often arrives wearing last week's disguise.

The Clerk's Salary

He complained that his pay was a pittance.
His boss, polishing profits, said: "You work as small as your wage."
The clerk looked at his hands—callused from cutting corners—and nodded.
He learned to measure effort by envelopes, not by hours.

Punchline: Wages mirror the size of the work we allow ourselves to do.

The Miser's Funeral

Relatives bawled that he left them nothing.
One cousin smiled and said: "He gave us work—we'll dig."
They argued over a will that read like a map to silence.
At the grave, the miser's fingers were empty even in death.

Punchline: The stingiest man finally paid—by absence.

The Miser's Lamp

He refused to light his lamp to "save oil."
Darkness saved his coins, but thieves saved their pockets.
One night he complained of shadows; the street outside glowed with other people's riches.
His thrift became someone else's profit.

Punchline: Saving on light costs someone else the night.

The Greedy River

The river widened each year, taking fields and fences alike.
Farmers wept as furrows were washed into memory.
The river said: "I return what you pour—your own tears and seeds."
One year it took a small temple; it returned only silence.

Punchline: Greed wears the current like a hungry tide.

The Beggar's Lottery

He scratched a ticket and fortune blinked open.
He bought a beautiful begging bowl and polished it every morning.
People admired the bowl more than his story.
He learned that style can be bought; dignity cannot.

Punchline: Even luck wants to look the part.

The Rich Man's Complaint

He moaned that money couldn't buy happiness.
A poor man, smiling with small hands, said: "Then lend me some."
The rich man counted reasons like coins, never spending them.
He discovered that unhappiness, like old silver, tarnishes slowly.

Punchline: Happiness doesn't come with a receipt, but money comes with excuses.

The Rich Widow

She sobbed loud and long at her husband's passing.
Her servant watched her tear the house into pieces, one sentence at a time.
"Your mourning costs nothing to the world, madam," the servant whispered.
One hand folded the will; the other folded her grief neatly into ledgers.

Punchline: Tears can be cheaper than an honest account.

The Rich Saint

He preached renunciation from a marble porch.
His plates were silver, his sandals silk, and his staff carved by artisans.
He told villagers the world was binding; he bound himself to comfort.
The cook mumbled: "He renounced on credit."

Punchline: Renunciation with a roof is a bestseller.

The Beggar's Wealth

Someone stole his worn blanket; he only smiled.
He said: "Even thieves are tired of stealing from me."
Neighbors shook their heads—pity was a heavier currency than kindness.
He slept warm in indifference.

Punchline: When even theft abandons you, you outlast appetite.

The Fake Saint

He fasted before crowds and feasted in secret.
Pilgrims drooled over his fasting face; backstage, he ate heartily.
He argued that God saw the heart; townsfolk looked to windows instead.
The altar smelled of perfume—an expensive kind of devotion.

Punchline: Public piety is often private appetite in costume.

The Lazy Saint

He claimed asceticism while ten servants changed his clothes.
"Renunciation," he said, "is a team sport."
He blessed the poor from a cushioned chair and measured faith by attendance.
People left offerings and left better dressed.

Punchline: Some saints outsource their sanctity.

The Hungry Saint

He lectured that hunger was illusion between sips of soup.
At night he ate three plates and told his disciples the taste was transcendence.
They believed him until they watched him close his eyes at the last bite.
Faith blurred when the stomach remembered.

Punchline: Illusions become very real around the dinner table.

The Drunken Monk

He preached purity in daylight and drank shadow by shadow at dusk.
Monks counted sins like beads; he counted wines like prayers.
He called it "testing your faith," and the temple called it "variety."
Believers forgave him because contradiction made scripture easier.
Punchline: Hypocrisy is the oldest sacrament of convenience.

The Talking Stone

A stone that had always been silent finally whispered a sentence.
Years had people talking to it and never hearing back.
When it spoke, listeners bent closer as if learning a long-forgotten vowel.
They realized they had spoken to a stone more than they listened to each other.

Punchline: Sometimes what finally answers is what we stopped expecting.

The Sleeping Saint

He slept through morning prayers and woke full of revelations.
"You dream faster to God," he told the scolding crowd.
They envied his restful piety; no one envied their own waking.
One priest watched the dreams and found sermons there he could not preach.
Punchline: Some devotions prefer the comfort of dreams.

The Temple Bell

The bell never rang; the priest praised the silence as proof of God's nearness.
Pilgrims left thinking silence was holiness and paid for it with incense.
A child asked why the bell slept; the priest said: "Use your ears for faith."
The bell, rusting in stillness, learned the price of being useful.

Punchline: Uselessness sometimes rebrands itself as sanctity.

The Crowded Temple

The temple filled with bodies more eager to be seen than to kneel.
The idol whispered to itself: "They came to prove they came."
Prayer lines turned into parades, devotion measured in footsteps.
When asked what they sought, many could only name the shrine's echo.

Punchline: Pilgrimage is often performance with better lighting.

The Broken Idol

A crack split the idol's face and villagers bowed deeper than before.
They said the flaw made it look more human, more reachable.
Repairmen were called; the idol was patched and left perfect again.
Devotion thinned when the face regained its distance.

Punchline: Flaws invite confession; perfection collects distances.

The Barber's Gossip

He trimmed beards and lives in half-measures, snipping confidences.
His scissors cut hair and reputations with equal skill.
He promised discretion but charged more for drama.
Clients left lighter but louder.

Punchline: Hair grows back; gossip roots deeper.

The Mocking God

A figure appeared in the square and told men to stop bothering him.
Surprised, one villager whispered: "At least prayer worked once."
People corrected their offerings; their loud bargains softened into private promises.
The apparition left; the market resumed its bargaining with a quieter voice.

Punchline: Even a god can tire of small talk.

The Ladder of Success

He climbed rung after rung thinking the top would open new skies.
At the end he found a wall and a view of other men still climbing.
He sat and told himself the journey was exercise—an attempt to justify sweat.
Climbers below took notes; climbers above took seats.

Punchline: Success builds ladders that often face walls.

The Fool's Lantern

He carried a lantern in full noon, searching for honest men.
Passersby laughed and showed their honesty in pockets and replies.
He declared himself unlucky: honesty hid from light.
Perhaps he was the one who needed to be lit.

Punchline: Some searches are the lanterns of the lost.

The Fool's Map

He sold a map to heaven, with routes and rest stops in gold ink.
Curious buyers asked why he still traded from the same town.
He said: "Maps guide others; sellers need roots."
Those who bought followed lines; the seller stayed, warm and unmoved.

Punchline: Guides often prefer customers to destinations.

The Fool's Crown

He made a crown from paper and declared himself monarch of light.
Children cheered; adults smirked; pigeons sat on his head like advisors.
He walked the streets with regal gestures; no taxes were collected.
His kingdom was thin air with a good hat.

Punchline: Paper crowns flutter louder than iron rule.

The Crowded Market

Merchants shouted bargains while buyers pushed to be first.
In the crush, people paid more to show they could afford less.
One beggar watched the market steal its own sense of cheapness.
He left with a coin, thinking wealth was a fever people bought.
Punchline: Markets sell the idea of value louder than value itself.

The Gossiping Parrot

A parrot repeated every scandal it heard in the town square.
Its names were ribbons tied to reputations; owners grew lonely.
When the parrot was sold, the town fell eerily silent—no scapegoat remained.
People missed the bird until they realized they shouldn't have taught it.

Punchline: Silence is only missed when noise stops being someone else's problem.

The Empty Jar

An empty jar clanged the loudest in the pantry.
Neighbors noticed its sound and thought the house fuller than before.
Voices, like jars, can make presence from absence.
The owner filled it with silence and sat content.

Punchline: Loudness is poor currency for content.

The Silent Drum

A boy beat a drum without rhythm and everyone said he'd be a great speaker.
He learned that noise can be interpreted as passion.
As he grew, speech replaced rhythm, and rhythm became excuse.
He discovered applause liked volume more than sense.

Punchline: Drums teach how to be heard; wisdom teaches whether to speak.

The Empty Purse

A thief returned an empty purse in anger—someone had already taken the joy.
A poor man said: "Even God returns prayers empty sometimes."
They both laughed at life's circular jokes.
The thief put the purse away and kept the lesson.

Punchline: Empty hands can carry pilgrimages too.

The Talking Wall

A wall that had heard secrets finally fell and spilled them into the street.
Neighbors read their own stories like torn letters on the ground.
Silence had been the wall's safest plaster; truth was its loose brick.
People learned that what holds up society can also hide rot.

Punchline: Walls keep secrets until they become ruins.

The Orator's Honesty

He spoke beautiful lines on truth from gilded stages.
Offstage, he practiced a dozen small deceits.
Listeners applauded the voice and forgave the hands.
Honesty became a speech delivered at intervals.

Punchline: Rhetoric can sound like virtue until someone asks for proof.

The Old Teacher

After forty winters of schooling others, he finally admitted ignorance.
Students blinked—were they being graded on skepticism?
He smiled: "At last I learned something from admitting I do not know."
They respected him more for the confession than for his lessons.

Punchline: Admission is the oldest classroom.

The Teacher's Cane

He used his cane to beat more than unruly boys; it became a staff of habit.
One day the cane cracked and didn't return.
The child who had been struck thanked the air—the pain had taught him more than the cane.
The cane, broken, whispered: "At least one of us got educated."

Punchline: Discipline breaks; lessons remain.

The Clever Student

He memorized pages as if knowledge were a harvest to be stored.
When life arrived with storms, his memory was full but his hands were empty.
Books kept him company while the world asked for warmth and courage.
He defended his grades and failed his days.

Punchline: Memory collects facts; life demands wisdom.

The Silent Poet

He burned his verses to protect readers from his vanity.
"Words corrupt silence," he told those who asked.
People hungered for his lines and learned the taste of absence.
His silence wrote its own poems in the town.

Punchline: Silence is a poem with no punctuation.

The Scholar's Library

Books piled like quiet mountains around his house.
Villagers said he had become part of his books—shelves replacing shoulders.
He read maps that led nowhere and histories that led back to him.
Knowledge, when hoarded, becomes a smaller world.

Punchline: A library can be a home or a hiding place.

The Scholar's Funeral

They praised his wisdom from the pulpit at his burial.
The graveyard echoed with words that once were written on his pages.
The coffin lay heavy with compliments that could not teach him to live longer.
Death sat the exam he could not revise for.

Punchline: Wisdom may bookend life, but it cannot stretch it.

The Silent Monk

Ten years he kept his vow of silence and grew like a lake—deep, still.
One night he shouted: "Finally free!" and the hillside echoed back eighty voices.
Silence had made him larger; sound merely proved it.
People realized the shout was the last echo of a long quiet.
Punchline: Silence fills rooms louder than any voice.

The Astrologer's Misfortune

He foretold births and rains, weddings and wars, with charts and candles.
The roof over his head collapsed one winter—no star warned him.
He patched it and wrote a new horoscope: "Customers first, fate later."
Villagers bought predictions and left their roofs to chance.
Punchline: Prophecy is good business until the house falls in.

The Tombstone Lie

His tombstone read: "He lived nobly."
A drunkard read it aloud and laughed: "He still lies."
People repeated the phrase as if polishing a memorial.
Truth at the grave becomes a civic ornament.

Punchline: Epitaphs are often hopeful fiction carved in stone.

The Final Lesson

A dying teacher said: "Life is short."
A student asked: "What about death?" and the teacher smiled: "Shorter."
They both laughed at the economy of time.
The lesson was simple and painfully timely.

Punchline: All tests end with the same bell.

The Talking Grave

At night the stones murmured the names they held.
Mourners shushed the earth as if it needed to be polite.
The dead's whispers were more honest than many living vows.
Villagers learned that the soil remembers what people forget.

Punchline: Graves keep conversations others abandon.

The Old Watch

An old watch stopped ticking and its owner sighed with relief.
"No more being late," he said, finally free of schedules it enforced.
He kept it in a drawer and told stories of time with a smile.
Sometimes the absence of ticking is a small, private rebellion.

Punchline: When the clock stops, life gets a line of free breathing.

The Farmer's Curse

He prayed for rain and cursed the mud when it arrived.
Neighbors said even God could not please such a man.
He wanted perfection and complained when nature complied with all its mess.
His fields grew stubborn under an ungrateful gaze.
Punchline: Blessings resent the critic's voice.

The Cow's Excuse

The cow gave less milk and blamed the weather and the watch.
"You drink tea, not milk," it seemed to say, as if manners guided udders.
The farmer scolded, the village joked, and the child went thirsty.
Sometimes excuses moo louder than facts.
Punchline: Animals can be honest when people invent reasons.

The Dancing Donkey

The donkey danced and brayed while the crowd laughed.
He thought the cheers were for his art; they were for the show.
When the laughter ceased, the donkey returned to work, pleased with applause that lasted minutes and debts that lasted seasons.
He had mistaken amusement for applause.

Punchline: Applause feeds vanity, not virtue.

The Crooked Tree

They spared the crooked tree because it could not fit the saw.
It grew twisted and wise, branches making room where others would break.
Birds nested in its odd hollows and children loved its peculiar shade.
Imperfection invited life.

Punchline: Flaws carve space for certain graces.

The Old Tree

It offered fruit and got stones.
People hurled complaints at roots that had fed generations.
The tree stood patient, dropping apples like small apologies.
Its shade kept giving long after gratitude had left.

Punchline: Generosity often pays back in unkindness.

The Proud Peacock

Its feathers shone until the rain came.
In drizzle they drooped, color bleeding to quiet.
A crow remarked: "Beauty drowns first," and the peacock learned humility.
Pride often forgets weather.

Punchline: Grace is fragile in a storm.

The Jealous Cat

It hated the dog, and lived on grudges.
When the dog died, the cat stopped eating—emptiness tasted like victory gone wrong.
Without its enemy, the world had less urge and less flavor.
The cat learned that hatred is a meal with no calories.

Punchline: Some appetites consume themselves when their object is gone.

The Clever Crow

It dropped pebbles and watched water rise in a pitcher.
When it saw its reflection, it flew away—wisdom beaten by vanity.
It chose the mirror's friend over thirst's prize.
Sometimes smart hands are lost to small glories.

Punchline: Wisdom is useful until self-love spoils the harvest.

The Lazy Dog

It barked at every stranger and slept when the chase came.
Neighbors said noise saved its energy and reputation.
It kept a roomy bed and an empty conscience.
In the end, the village measured courage in deeds, not decibels.

Punchline: Noise is a sleepy dog's autobiography.

The Hungry Cat

Each morning it stole the monk's milk and purred in repentance.
The monk laughed and said: "At least someone worships regularly."
The cat grew fat on rituals and rats alike.
Devotion sometimes travels on four paws.

Punchline: Daily worship keeps hunger polite.

The Foolish Rat

It stole grain and prayed for better luck.
God, if listening, shrugged—thieves have their own prayers.
The rat's tiny faith was equal parts hunger and hope.
Sometimes mischief invents piety to sleep easier.

Punchline: Prayer is the last refuge of the petty.

The Honest Shopkeeper

His sign read "We sell truth" and the shelves were nearly empty.
He added "We sell lies too" and suddenly the shop was busy.
People came for stories with warranties and left with dusty honesty.
He learned that trade prefers variety.

Punchline: Truth without choice is a poor merchant.

The Loud Beggar

He cried hunger in the square but hid bread under his robe.
His shouts bought him sympathy in quarters and suspicion in whole coins.
He liked the taste of attention more than the food he denied himself.
Performance paid better than meals.

Punchline: Hunger sounds better when amplified.

The Village Idiot

Lost often in card games, he kept a circle of loyal friends.
Where clever men plotted, he laughed with those who remained.
His poverty of guile made him rich in company.
People noticed that games keep people close; cunning keeps them apart.

Punchline: Simplicity buys friendship the market cannot price.

The Barber's Half-Beard

He cut a man's beard half to prove a point about half-lives.
The man left, half-shaved and whole in indignation.
The barber said: "Most men live half-lives anyway."
The mirror reflected two halves neither wanted to meet.

Punchline: Partial truths leave faces uneven.

The Lazy Gardener

He planted weeds where flowers required patience.
They grew faster, looked like neighbors' blooms, and required little care.
People admired his "natural" garden and secretly weeded the rest.
Laziness sometimes cultivates an easy kind of beauty.

Punchline: Neglect grows things that look

The Minister's Chair

He clung to the chair tighter than to his conscience.
When asked why, he replied: "The chair has legs; conscience doesn't."

Punchline: Power rests where wood is stronger than will.

The King's Ears

Flatterers shouted praise into the king's ears until he went deaf.
Doctors said his hearing was gone; courtiers said his wisdom had grown.

Punchline: Silence sounds like wisdom when no one dares the truth.

The Ruler's Statue

He built his statue taller than his palace.
One day a crow perched on the head and dirtied it.

Punchline: Even stone rulers get crowned by crows.

The Court Poet

He praised the king as divine in every verse.
The king asked: "Why divine?"
Poet replied: "God too cannot be questioned."

Punchline: Flattery is safest when it wears theology.

The Soldier's Sword

He sharpened it daily, though no war was near.
Asked why, he smiled: "Peace makes me unemployed."

Punchline: Some men live only when death works.

The Banker's Vault

He locked gold in chests and threw away the key.
When he died, no one could open them.

Punchline: His greatest savings was his family's greatest loss.

The Greedy Farmer

He hoarded grain until rats worshipped him like a god.
Villagers starved outside while the rats sang hymns inside.

Punchline: Greed always finds worshippers, never neighbors.

The Miser's Shoes

He never wore them, afraid they'd wear out.
At death, they looked new—unlike his feet.

Punchline: He saved leather, but lost his journey.

The Merchant's Scales

He tilted them cleverly, weighing profit heavier than fairness.
One day the scales broke.

Punchline: Justice weighs itself when iron snaps.

The Jewel Thief

He stole gems and hid them under his bed.
Each night he dreamt of being robbed.

Punchline: Fear becomes the heaviest jewel.

The Preacher's Purse

He thundered against wealth on Sundays.
On Mondays, he counted donations.

Punchline: Sin funds many sermons.

The Holy River

Pilgrims bathed to wash sins.
The river whispered: "You leave sins here, but carry them back."

Punchline: Water cleanses skin, not memory.

The Prophet's Shoes

He walked barefoot to prove humility.
Disciples carried golden slippers behind him "just in case."

Punchline: Even humility collects a treasury.

The Saint's Shadow

People bowed to his shadow, not him.
The saint laughed: "You worship darkness around light."

Punchline: Devotion often mistakes outline for essence.

The Temple Beggar

He begged at the temple gates, richer in coins than shopkeepers.
When asked why he stayed, he smiled: "Faith pays daily."

Punchline: Piety fills bowls faster than labor.

The Fool's Well

He dropped a coin into the well for luck.
When it didn't return, he threw another.

Punchline: Superstition is the well that never refunds.

Epilogue

The stories in 'The Unheard' were never meant to end; they were meant to return. Like ripples in a pond, they spread, fade, and then reappear as questions in the reader's own reflection. Every fable here carries a twin — its silence. The words are temporary; their stillness is what remains.

I have often thought of wisdom not as accumulation but as subtraction — the slow shedding of pretensions until what remains is simple and transparent. Each story was a small act of erasure: less doctrine, more presence; fewer explanations, more seeing. In that sense, 'The Unheard' is not a book to be finished, but a light house to be revisited.

We live in an age that measures truth by visibility — by what trends, what is liked, what glows on a screen. Yet the deeper truths are shy; they live in shadows, in pauses, in moments we overlook. The parables in this collection are reminders that meaning is not always loud. Sometimes, the quietest thought carries the longest echo. That is what 'The Unheard' is.

When I imagine these stories scattered into the world, I see them not as printed lines but as seeds carried by wind — some will fall on laughter, some on doubt, some on silence. Wherever they land, may they bloom into understanding.

And if nothing blooms, may they at least make you smile before the next sunrise.

For ultimately, wisdom is not about solving life; it is about smiling at its mystery.

Dr. Kumud Ramanand Bansal

Be in love with life